The National Best Selling Author,

Dale L. Roberts

by Ben Gothard,

Founder & CEO of Gothard Enterprises LLC

Author of CEO at 20: A Little Book for Big Dreams

Project EGG

ENTREPRENEURS GATHERING FOR GROWTH

Project EGG is an elite network of entrepreneurs, authors & incredible people who problem solve, bounce ideas off of each other, share their stories and succeed together.

This mastermind includes people from around the world who are making a difference right now. We have a truly incredible group of people, like CEOs, CFOs, founders, national best-selling authors, inventors, marketers, coaches, consultants, musicians, speakers, and many many more entrepreneurs from every corner of the globe.

In the official Project EGG podcast, hosted by myself, Ben Gothard, different members of the group are interviewed. Each interview is a deep-dive into the life of the guest as both the guest and I drill down into entrepreneurship and personal development. By sharing their life and experiences, we can all learn something valuable.

This book is a transcription of the interview, unedited. Hopefully you can get as much out of the interview as I did hosting it!

Connect with Dale:

YouTube:

https://www.youtube.com/channel/UCKv8xcrFntOERL7NUXgkypg

Amazon: http://amzn.to/2mjder1

Facebook:

https://www.facebook.com/authordalelroberts

Ben: Hello, everybody. Thanks for tuning in and listening. Today, we're going to be talking to Dale L. Roberts from Columbus, Ohio. Dale, you want to introduce yourself?

Dale: Yeah, hey, well I think that you pretty much covered it. I'm Dale L. Roberts. I am an avid shuffleboard enthusiast, self-published author, number one best-selling internationally-speaking, and I'm definitely not the Batman.

Ben: Alright, that's awesome. Well thanks for tuning in with us today, Dale. So I guess let's jump right into it. The first question I have for you today is: what is your story?

Dale: Wow. Oh man. This might cover about an hour here so I hope we got some time.

Ben: Please.

Dale: But in any event, I'm actually one of three children in a military family. My mother was in the Navy; my father was in the Marine Corps. Growing up, it was primarily my father who was in the military because my mother had already been out of service by the time I was already born. I was able to travel the world at a very young age. I believe I lived a very privileged life. So there were many experiences that I got at a very early age that not anybody could probably get the rest of their life. I'd always really... I've been a bit... when I was growing up, I was an introvert. I loved reading—that was one thing that I just absolutely I could just... that was my escape. I would just sit and I would read—play video games, of course, what kid doesn't play video games—and eventually got to the point where I enjoyed reading so much I started creating my own stories.

So, we fast-forward some time later as I was going through school, I decided that was going to be what I was going to go to college for—become a writer. I had my mind set on becoming a writer for Guitar World Magazine. Never came to fruition because I got to college and I just discovered really quickly that writing is not for sissies, I'm telling you what, man—especially if you're going to school, specifically for that. I mean, my very first class, I think our first paper that was handed in and I think I got an F. It pretty much, this guy was like, no focus, everything's all over the place. You got bad grammar, syntax, everything else in-between and I pretty much tail tucked ran off and thankfully my aunt had helped me out. Really cleaned up things and I was able to go through about two semesters and really do pretty well in college because of her.

But I just eventually just kind of lost sight of things, became very defeated and I got into a heavy metal band. That's when I really started focusing on just music, music, music. When I get on something I really focus and I get very obsessive on it. We became mildly successful; we're able to get all over just the Midwest area. Made a little bit of scratch on the side part-time. Meanwhile, I worked as an activities director in the healthcare industry. So essentially, I got paid to play with senior citizens.

Let's chop this up here hopefully because I'll just be bloviating after a while. I fell in love with professional wrestling. 1999, August 1999. I just happened to be flipping through the channels and I got hooked. Mind you, as a kid, I was always told it was the F-word—it was fake. I just never paid attention to it. It wasn't until my adult life that I actually started watching it and I became hooked and that's when I became so obsessed about watching it, and of course watching it, I saw all these athletes and I wanted to be just like them. So that's why I started to really gravitate towards health and fitness — getting myself in better shape, getting rid of this little potbelly that I got over the years of drinking alcohol and everything else in-between.

Eventually, I went to some crappy local gym to get trained in professional wrestling and I took it so seriously that eventually I ended up getting a tryout with other WWF at the time, WWE now — people over in Louisville, Kentucky. And that's when I said, okay, this is it, this is great but I eventually said, okay, if I'm going to take this really seriously — because WWF wasn't interested in hiring me because I didn't know my ass from a hole in the ground. So I ended up going over to Calgary, Alberta, Canada and I trained underneath Lance Storm, former WWE superstar, multiple title-holder, things like that and I got into wrestling.

I promise you, I'm getting to the end of this story here. This does get better, it does lead up to what I'm going to talk about and that is eventually, I got a serious injury. It screwed my back up. I went from being a solid 220, muscled-out and everything else like that to shriveling down to about 175, or right about 175 or 180 right now. That back injury really screwed me up and I had to get out of wrestling. I stuck around doing the work and activities all that time.

It's been twenty years in healthcare industry but in the back of my mind, writing kept nagging at me and that's where I finally got a little bit of coaxing from some people and actually wrote my very first book about three years ago. And the funny thing is, it made me some money and that's where pretty much self-publishing comes into play. When I started realizing it could make me money, that's when I realized do I really need a day job? Now, this is something I tell everybody. Don't do what I did. I literally burned the boats a little too soon. Thankfully, my wife was running a very good Amazon FBA business and we were making a significant amount of income on that.

But other than that though, the self-publishing, I bailed on my job pretty much to get $20 paychecks per month up to $200 paychecks so you can only imagine how tough it was for a while. We really struggled for a while; I got used to eating ramen noodles. It wasn't until actually I looked into getting an actual self-publishing course through Jason Bracht and also further mentoring with him—I got coaching through him—that I was able to take my business from down here, low-level, to functioning at a much higher level. I'll tell you what, he blew my mind and he really expanded the business and got me to where I am today. So that's my story, now that we're out of time, thank you everybody for tuning in... No, I'm just kidding.

Ben: That's great. I just have a few questions about your past. You said you grew up with a military family on both sides. Do you think growing up in that sort of household kind of implanted certain values in you that have helped you succeed and if so, what values were they?

Dale: Absolutely. I was in a bit of a different military situation. Sometimes people would say, well I was in a military family, so you almost get this picture of like a drill sergeant father with a crew cut that would be very demanding—sit up straight, answer yes or yes, Ma'am—so at a certain extent yeah, we were very disciplined. But to a certain extent, I think that it was really my mother was the disciplinarian; my father, being the Marine Corps you would think he would've been the drill sergeant type person but actually he was the person I got my sense of humor from. He's the cut-up, he's the joker, always has something funny, rarely ever in a bad mood. Everybody loved Mike Roberts. I learned how to be professional but at the same instance I learned how to be fun.

So it was the mixture of both parents. Their undying work ethic; that was one thing they really passed down to me. It was never anything they ever said to me. It was just kind of led by example. When you work on something, you put your heart into it—whether you're scrubbing a toilet or you're serving a burger to somebody at McDonald's—just any line of work, you should take pride in it because it represents who you are as a person. That's why I do what I do with all the heart and all the passion and every bit of energy inside my soul is put into what I do. I think I was very fortunate and it really does play a large part in how I'm able to do my business, how I do function on a day-to-day basis. Hopefully that answered your question. I'm not really 100% sure that's what you're looking for.

Ben: Absolutely. Now, you said a little bit after talking about your family how you got to travel and you got to see a lot of different things and you got to be exposed to different cultures. Do you think that because of your travels, you have a better perspective on both yourself and life in general from those travels?

Dale: Absolutely. Being exposed to numerous cultures and different portions of the United States. Living in Japan for three years—when I was ten to thirteen years old—was an amazing experience. I mean, that was... I don't think I could trade that for the world. That was one of the best portions of my life course. I say that a lot about my portions of life, but that right there was the most memorable because it was such a beautiful country and such a wonderful culture over in Japan. I think that really helped to mold me and make me probably a little bit more mature at a younger age.

Ben: Do you think that because you got to travel that it helped you get more comfortable talking to other people and you kind of learned how to be comfortable even when you're uncomfortable? Do you think that plays a part of your success?

Dale: That could be a large part of it but the funny thing is, I probably didn't start developing into more of an extrovert till I was later into high school. My father already had an honorable discharge in 1989 so we moved to Ohio, in Attica—small, small town—my grandma lived there; my aunt and her family had lived out there; my uncle lived nearby. Ohio was a good fit for the Roberts family. We ended up settling down once he was out of the military. When I went to high school, that's pretty much where I picked up and we'd moved up from Japan in '89 over to the middle of nowhere in Attica, Ohio. That's really—I'm bloviating, I can tell already—this is great. I run into this problem on Bootstrap businessmen. What was the question again, I'm sorry?

Ben: When you were travelling and you're getting to talk to different people—

Dale: Oh, extrovert. Yes. Didn't become an extrovert till I was in high school. It took a while for me to open up. I became good at speaking, believe it or not, because I was doing a gig called Voice of Democracy in high school. It was because of the urging of my Social Studies teacher—who's now since passed, his name was

Mr. Brenaman—he took me aside and he just told me, you know, he really kind of fluffed my ego where he's just like, I really see there's a lot of promise in you, I think you should do this, and he said the thing that most interested me—wasn't the fact that I could be able to talk patriotically about my country—but it was the prize money that was involved. He was just like, you know there's going to be—I can't remember, probably was like $50 on the contest—and I was like, I'm in. It was very uncomfortable at first. Yes, I will admit to you. I'm shaking, I'm nervous, and I don't think I shook that feeling even going into a rock band and being in front of people. I was always just—I'd get the jitters.

Fast-forward some time later though, when I got into pro-wrestling, I had no issues in getting in front of an audience. Someone will hand me a microphone and it was like a trigger and I would just all of a sudden, I just felt like nerves would go completely away. The funny thing is, you could sit me down with one person one-on-one and sometimes I'll get nervous. I don't know what the deal is, but you put me in front of a group of hundreds of people and I'm at peace. I'm not really sure; it could be years of working with senior citizens—hosting parties, major events, things like that—where it was in my mindset that well, they don't pay me to be nervous. I just eventually just I got rid of a lot of those inhibitions, those things at the back of my head that I think they call it like a monkey mindset where it's just like, you're not good enough to talk and I just eventually got in front of people and I felt comfortable. Man, I'm so glad you rescued me on that question right there I just start going off on a tangent there. I think it's time to re-up on my coffee, man.

Ben: So I kind of want to talk about your days in the heavy metal band scene. First of all, what did you play and what did you really get out of it? What was your biggest value that you got from being in that?

Dale: I played lead guitar, primarily. I usually butchered up most lead guitar things. Eventually got into actually singing/screaming in a band since it's a metal band. The biggest thing that I got from it was I learned that I put the bar way too high on the people I surrounded myself with because I expected a lot of myself so what I would end up doing was I became a bit of a dictator, bit of a control freak and sometimes, you become friends with the people that you're inside this band but it really alienated me from people that I considered friends. I really ruined quite a few friendships from that control freak type nature I had. It actually started to teach me that sure, you can hold people at a high expectation, but you got to also make sure that they know that those expectations are set and they agree to those expectations.

As an example, had a bass player, he was my best buddy. We ended up—we're actually roommates for a number of years—and come to find out he was doing some drugs he shouldn't have been doing. We're not talking like smoking pot; we're talking like the hardcore stuff and I confronted him on it. The issue I ran into was I told him once, great. Second time it happens and I confronted him again and that time he said, look, promise won't do it again. But unfortunately, I felt like it was too little too late at that point and I was influenced in a way by the drummer that hey look, you already put that out there, and I ended up firing him. It literally destroyed a friendship.

It's one thing if a person was an addict and they were stealing from us or doing things wrong, but at this point he was just recreationally abusing drugs. Abusing not like he was snorting rails off of hookers or anything else like that but it was enough that it was, in my opinion, something that could really endanger his life which in turn means that we'd have to fill his position so we just said screw it, you're out of here. It really sucks. So that was one of the biggest things I learned was, don't just secretly set expectations for people that you surround yourself with. You need to be very vocal and you need to be straightforward and upfront and also be very tactful about your expectations and you got to make sure that they agree to those expectations because just because you have those doesn't necessarily mean they agree with them.

Ben: Right, that's a really good point. So kind of moving a little bit chronologically past the band scene, you said at some point you kept feeling this nagging, this intuition for writing. What was the tipping point that you said, okay, I'm going to start writing now and do you wish you would've started sooner?

Dale: Well first of all, yes, I really wish I had started sooner. The only reason why I hadn't— and I think a lot of people can relate to this—is there are ton of people. They always say this and it's funny; they poke fun at the cartoon The Family Guy with the dog and you just say, I'm going to write this book someday. There's going to be this book. You got this idea in your head and you just—you always kind of say, oh I'm going to write this book and for the longest time as a personal trainer—which I was a personal trainer for a cup of coffee—and at that time, I really kept saying all this information I've got, I would love to just put it to a book so then I could just hand it to my client be like, read this, come back to me, and I'll start training you. It was kind of a joke at first but eventually I'm just kind of like, man, I really do need to sit down and do that. But my thought was, cause at that time, I started training in about 2006 and as you may know, it really didn't start blowing up—the e-book business hadn't started really expanding to about 2008, 2009—and I could be off on my date so please anybody that's out there like, technically. Look, just go with me on this story.

Ben: Or let us know in the comments.

Dale: Yes, let us know in the comments, absolutely. So in any event, 2006, I started doing the training and I was doing that from about 2006 to 2010, 2011ish at a chain gym in Columbus. It was already kind of on my mind to create a book. It wasn't until I was actually out here in Phoenix, Arizona and I was working at an assisted living community, we had what was called a wellness coach. Well this wellness coach said you're just like the easiest person to work with. She never had to tell me you have to eat healthier. She's like…you eat healthy? I don't know what I can tell you to eat more of. So you just kind of like you know so how's your work outs been? I'm like, great, awesome, I'll tell you I do like a hundred to a thousand squats. It's just a wrestler mentality where I would just continually try to improve myself physically speaking.

She started coming up with different things where she challenged me to meditate more and then it came out that I liked writing. She was like, so what have you wrote? I'm like well, I hadn't written anything yet and when it came out, I'm like, oh hell. She's going to use this against me! Sure enough, that was one of my goals. She said, okay, why don't you write a book? And I'm like, yeah, I've always thought about that. Well, after the second time of her bringing up the whole book thing, I was like, fine, okay I'll do it. I'll do it. So I started getting up around 4 AM—and we're talking I got up at

4 AM for probably I think it had to have been about three months straight—and I would work for about an hour to two hours just wildly typing. Literally, I had no outline; all I did was I would just sit there and I would just talk about all the things involved in fitness and that eventually came out to what is now out in the market called The Three Keys to Greater Health and Happiness. Now, it wasn't called that originally—it was a different name, it was poorly edited, but the bottom line is, I did finish it.

I did put it out and when I put it out and made some money, that's when I was like, this is awesome. So it was really my wellness coach who held me up to a higher standard and really kind of put the flame underneath my ass to say, get going, let's do this. It's always great to have somebody like that—somebody to cheer you on. If you're ever a person who has a book within you and you find you're kind of hitting a sticking point, I would just say it's kind of like working out. Get yourself a partner; someone who holds you accountable so that way, they can come back and say, hey, how's that book going? Did you get ten pages written over the last week? That really helped me out a lot, so hugely, hugely thankful and actually, I think I even thanked her in my first book.

Ben: That's great, and that kind of actually leads perfectly into my next question. You mentioned your wellness coach and Lance Storm, I believe as mentors to you and also Jason Bracht, if I remember correctly. Could you point to any other people who have significantly helped or mentored you and how they were instrumental in your success?

Dale: Oh man, you got mentors and you got leaders around you all the time and sometimes they come in the weirdest form. I would say that—this is a tough question to answer—how about I do this, because I have told you the most positive ones, the ones you could look at and say man, they're successful, and so I want to model that success. Dewan Bayney is another great one. He actually interviewed me early on this year and I was thrilled to actually be able to talk to Dewan. I was exposed to Dewan Bayney through Jason Brock because he'd interviewed him the year prior and I just started following Dewan; I thought this guy's the man. But why don't I just go ahead and I'm going to do something a little different so what I'll do is I'll tell you a different type of a mentor — different type of a leader — a person that starts to teach you things.

I worked with this person. I'm not going to name any names. She was a very foul person. She was not happy with her life. She hated her husband. She didn't like her job and it was very clear. And I had to work with this woman on a daily basis. I did not like being around her. I didn't like her attitude; I didn't like the way she treated people. And it got to the point where I even complained to my direct manager and I felt like it was going unanswered. It was like, well, that's kind of like the way she is, why don't we sit down and we'll have a chat. I'm like, no. Other than painting the reptile, you can't change the snake's skin; a snake will always be a snake, will always be snake.

I'm going to a job to try to fulfill my obligation and make a living, but here I was—I was going to the job and I was miserable. I was just so unhappy because I would have to end up working with this person. But then when I started to realize I'm like, wait a second, I really don't have to do this. And she was kind of a person that was put in my path—I believe—to show me what I should not do in life. Because I'm sure if I were to stayed into my job, I would've continued to be miserable. I would've chosen to be miserable and then eventually I would have ended up being like her. So she was a teacher. She was a mentor in a different regard. It was a way that you probably shouldn't do it this way. You hear that quite a bit—some people point out, get a mentor, get a coach, get a teacher, but sometimes they're right around you every single opportunity that you have. Even my exposure with you, Ben, that's going to be a learning experience—not that it's going to be anything like this bad person that I used to worked with—but every single experience is just vital. You just have to be very receptive to it. That's the thing. Always learn, always ask questions, always be hungry to learn more. Just because something's bad doesn't mean it's not going to teach you something good.

Ben: Right, that's a great point. So moving forward, we kind of touched on your past, we kind of talked about where you are and how you got there and who helped you get there. What would you say, moving forward, is the one biggest thing that you would like to accomplish in your lifetime?

Dale: That's so tough to say. I have crossed-off a lot of big goals—making a significant income that can support my wife and I is huge, huge to me. I would like to eventually get it to the point where—man, that's a loaded question. That's a good one. I'm just going to speak off the cuff here so hopefully nobody holds this to me but I would like to eventually get it to the point where I don't just make a good successful living but I want to get it to where I can explore the world with my wife and not have to necessarily worry about the financial constraints. In other words, if I wanted to jump off this call — which I could, technically, do that right now, wouldn't be a good idea — but as soon as I jump off this call, be nice if I said to my wife, you know what, let's go to Venice and it wouldn't be an issue.

Could we do it right now? Yes. Could we afford it? Probably not.

And the same instance I want to be able to get it to where I can be able to financially handle most anything for travel — because travelling with my wife is one of the most fun things for me. I love going and spending time with her. We're going to be going to Puerto Rico here soon and that's going to be a first experience for the both of us. I can't wait, I'm ecstatic about it. So I want to have that option and that availability to do that. So I want to have that option and that availability to do that. You're going to get a lot of people that will say, well I want world peace; I want to solve hunger, things like that. Well, of course everybody wants to have those types of humanitarian efforts. Adding that in there, barring that, putting that aside, essentially I would like to eventually get to where I can just travel the world, unencumbered by any financial constraints.

Ben: That's great. I have two more questions for you, if you don't mind.

Dale: Sure. Hey, take your time.

Ben: So the first question is: if you could give one piece of advice that would serve as your legacy, what would it be?

Dale: One piece of advice that could serve as my legacy. Man. This is great because this is probably going to be like a quote that's going to end up being put somewhere. Either someone's going to laugh at or they're going to go with it. Whatever you do, make sure it makes you happy. That's not at the expense of somebody else's happiness but it's so important that you smile more, that you laugh more, and that you surround yourself with people with that same purpose. Be happy, laugh a lot, because the thing is, you never know if tomorrow's going to come to you. A lot of people live their lives like they think, tomorrow, I'm going to do that, I want to be here. They can think they're going to be living forever, they think they're immortal.

The thing is, you don't know if that's going to happen. Going back to the being miserable in your job, going every day—that sucked for me that I chose to be unhappy. And now that I know I can be happy any day I want to, it's the most freedom that I can have. That one bit of advice I can share with people is man, be happy. Just two words, it's all you need. Be happy. It's going to be easier said than done for some of your listeners. Some people are like, I'm not happy; I hate my husband or I hate my wife and my children cost me thousands of dollars per month.

Well, clearly I had the choice of an exit strategy at my job, but if you got wife and kids and you're not happy around or anything else like that, then there's something needs to change—and that doesn't necessarily mean that you need to leave your family but you need to probably make some different decisions and some different internal choices. That is my legacy. If I were to have it on my tombstone — which hopefully there won't be any tombstones for me, I think that's just a waste of valuable earth space, donate me to science — but if I were to have on my virtual tombstone, it would be, at least he was happy.

Ben: That's great. For the last question, I just want to ask: is there anything that you think is an important part of who you are and are an important part of your story that I didn't ask you about today?

Dale: You asked a lot of really good lit questions. It's so funny. I almost—any time I get interviewed, I wait for that one question which is, how much are you making per month? What was your best month? And it's so funny and you probably see this on Self-Publishing with Dale L. Roberts over on my YouTube channel, eventually. I'm sorry if this is going to be slightly vulgar, Ben, please forgive me and anybody who listens to this; talking about your income is like working and you got somebody who's sitting by the water cooler bragging about their price per hour. It's like a dick measuring contest. I'm sure there are some people like, I don't say it to brag, well, why are you saying it? Don't share with me your stuff.

It's just amazes me. I did thirty thousand dollars per month and yadda yadda... well, whoop dee doo. You could be making so much money per month and if you're making this much money per month, can I ask you a question is, how happy are you? How wealthy are you truly in spirit? Are you very rich or do you just have like a really large bank account because doesn't make a damn difference to me. There's lots of millionaires and billionaires out there that are miserable sons of guns but I'll tell you this much; I am more wealthy than anyone of them put together, because the fact that I don't need a dollar sign per month that I did. It all comes down to this whole thing of just let's see, everybody just flop their thing out, let's go ahead and measure each one of our sizes. Does it really matter at the end of the day? Are you really thinking you're inspiring somebody by sharing the fact that you made thirty thousand dollars, sixty thousand dollars and yadda yadda.

I would say to the person that says to me, you know what, I'm successful. Why are you successful? Tell me those measurable things that don't include a dollar sign, that's going to inspire me. That right there just gives me goosebumps. People that get to realize life goals that are outside of the financial constraints, that right there is amazing to me. So kudos to you that you didn't bring up that question because I would've probably ended up shooting that one down because it just kills me. I had a podcast with my friend Kevin called Bootstrap Businessmen. We had interviewed Dewan—before we got on with Dewan, Dewan just like I got one request guys. Sure, fire away. He's like, could you not ask like the financial situation? I'm like, wasn't going to touch it. We're on the same boat on that one and it was so wonderful. You've done a great job; I really think that you've covered a lot of things. It's been a lot of fun. I don't know if there's anything else I can be able to help you out as far as any kind of questions I can cover—I'm more than happy to—and it's obviously been really awesome.

Ben: Yeah well, I guess if we think of more of questions or the listeners have any more questions, we can always maybe do a follow-up interview later on down the road.

Dale: I'd be happy to. Yeah, it's always a blast and if there's anything I can ever do, please reach out to me guys. I think Ben, you can probably be testimonial that I'm very approachable and I keep myself somewhat available so you can always look for me on Facebook: Dale L. Roberts. It's very simple to find me, I've got like a picture of me shrugging at I think like weights or something like that.

Ben: Alright. Well, everybody this is Dale L. Roberts from Columbus, Ohio. Thank you so much for tuning in and have a great day.

www.ingramcontent.com/pod-product-compliance
Lightning Source LLC
Chambersburg PA
CBHW070955280326
41934CB00009B/2069